Purpose
for
Everyday Living

for
Teachers

Simon & Schuster, Inc.
1230 Avenue of the Americas, New York, NY 10020

Freeman-Smith, LLC.

Nashville, TN 37202

The quoted ideas expressed in this book (but not Scripture verses) are not, in all cases, exact quota-
tions, as some have been edited for clarity and brevity. In all cases, the author has attempted to
maintain the speaker's original intent. In some cases, quoted material for this book was obtained
from secondary sources, primarily print media. While every effort was made to ensure the accuracy
of these sources, the accuracy cannot be guaranteed. For additions, deletions, corrections, or clari-
fications in future editions of this text, please write Freeman-Smith, LLC.

Scripture quotations marked MSG are taken from THE MESSAGE. Copyright
© 1993, 1994, 1995, 1996, 2000, 2001, 2002. Used by permission of NavPress
Publishing Group.

Scripture quotations marked NASB are taken from the NEW AMERICAN
STANDARD BIBLE, © 1960, 1962, 1963, 1968, 1971, 1972, 1973, 1975, 1977,
by The Lockman Foundation. Used by permission.

Scripture quotations marked NCV are taken from the New Century Version®.
Copyright © 1987, 1988, 1991 by Thomas Nelson, Inc. Used by permission.
All rights reserved.

Scripture quotations marked NIV are taken from the HOLY BIBLE, NEW
INTERNATIONAL VERSION®. Copyright © 1973, 1978, 1984 by Inter-
national Bible Society. Used by permission of Zondervan Publishing House.
All rights reserved.

Scripture quotations marked NKJV are taken from The Holy Bible, New
King James Version. Copyright © 1982, 1988 by Thomas Nelson, Inc. All
rights reserved.

Scripture quotations marked NLT are taken from the Holy Bible, New Living
Translation, copyright © 1996. Used by permission of Tyndale House Publishers, Inc., Wheaton, Illinois 60189. All rights reserved.

Scripture quotations marked HCSB have been taken from the Holman Christian Standard Bible®, copyright © 1999, 2000, 2002, 2003 by Holman Bible
Publishers. Used by permission.

Scriptures marked KJV are taken from the *Holy Bible, King James Version.*

Cover Design & Page Layout by Bart Dawson

Manufactured in the United States of America

10 9 8 7 6 5 4 3

ISBN-13: 978-1-4169-4841-4
ISBN-10: 1-4169-4841-4

Purpose
for
Everyday Living

for
Teachers

Simon & Schuster, Inc.
NEW YORK LONDON TORONTO SYDNEY

Table of Contents

Introduction

Henry Adams correctly observed, "A teacher affects eternity; he can never tell where his influence stops." Never have those words been more appropriate. We live in a difficult, fast-paced, temptation-filled world; more than ever, our young people need the direction and the leadership provided by teachers who know and love God.

God has a plan for everything, including you. Whether you teach graduate school or Sunday School, whether you lecture at seminary or at Vacation Bible School, your Creator is working in you and through you to help mold the minds and shape the hearts of your students. As preparation for this important task, you need and deserve a regularly scheduled conference with the ultimate Teacher. After all, you are God's emissary; He takes your teaching duties very seriously, and so should you.

So, if you are fortunate enough to find yourself in the role of teacher, accept a hearty congratulations and a profound word of thanks. And then, take a few moments each morning to consider the promises and prayers on these pages. Remember that God honors your profession just as surely as He offers His loving abundance to you and your students. With God's help, you are destined to reshape eternity. It's a big job, but don't worry: you and God, working together, can handle it.

Chapter 1

Discovering God's Purpose

You will show me the path of life;
in Your presence is fullness of joy;
at Your right hand are pleasures forevermore.
Psalm 16:11 NKJV

God has a plan for all of us, students and teachers alike. As a teacher, you bear a special responsibility for training the students who are entrusted to your care. Because of your position as a guide and mentor, you must be especially careful to seek God's will and to follow it.

God will not force His will upon you. To the contrary, He has given you the free will to follow His commandments . . . or not. If you stray from those commandments, you invite bitter consequences. But, when you choose to follow Him by genuinely and humbly seeking His will, God will touch your heart and lead you on the path of His choosing.

God intends to use you in wonderful, unexpected ways *if* you let Him, but be forewarned: the decision to seek God's plan and fulfill His purpose is yours and yours alone. The consequences of that decision have profound implications for you *and* your students, so choose carefully. And then, as you enter the classroom, rest assured that God intends to lead you and use you as a powerful tool for good. Your challenge

is to watch for His signs, to obey His
commandments, and to follow His path.

———

You are God's chief creation, and you are
here for His pleasure and His glory.

Beth Moore

We aren't just thrown on this earth like
dice tossed across a table.
We are lovingly placed here for a purpose.

Charles Swindoll

You cannot stay where you are and go with
God. You cannot continue doing things
your way and accomplish God's purposes in
His ways. Your thinking cannot come close
to God's thoughts. For you to do the will of
God, you must adjust your life to Him,
His purposes, and His ways.

Henry Blackaby

Open Yourself Up to God

Perhaps you have been overly anxious to impose your own plans upon the world. If so, it's time to open yourself up to God. If you have been struggling against God's will for your life, you have invited unwelcome consequences into your own life *and* into the lives of your loved ones. A far better strategy is to consult God earnestly and consistently *before* you embark upon the next stage of your life's journey.

Chapter 2

Purpose Through Teaching

In every way be an example of doing good deeds.
When you teach,
do it with honesty and seriousness.

Titus 2:7 NCV

The messages that we teach and the lives that we lead can have a profound impact upon our students. All of us remember teachers who greatly influenced our own lives. Now, it's our turn.

In the classroom, our purpose is clear: we must ensure that the messages we share with our students are sound, practical, and true. The ultimate truth, of course, is found in the Word of God through the person of His Son, Jesus. And even if Bible teachings are not a formal part of a school's curriculum, God's Word should be firmly planted in the heart of every Christian who teaches there.

Our students need encouraging mentors and worthy role models. As we stand before our students each day, we teach "what we know" *and* "who we are." And make no mistake: our students will see us for who we *really* are and what we *really* believe. Let us teach—and live—accordingly.

Teaching is a divine
calling. Whether we teach
at home, at church,
or in a school classroom,
transfer of knowledge is
a significant undertaking.

–

Suzanne Dale Ezell

In a completely rational society, the best
of us would aspire to be teachers
and the rest of us would have to settle for
something less, because passing civilization
along from one generation to the next
ought to be the highest honor and
the highest responsibility anyone could have.

Lee Iacocca

What could be more important than
equipping the next generation with
the character and competence
they need to become successful.

Colin Powell

If you have knowledge,
let others light their candles at it.

Margaret Fuller

Teaching was the hardest work
I had ever done, and it remains
the hardest work I have done to date.

Ann Richards

I touch the future.
I teach.

—

Christa McAuliffe

Let us look upon our children; let us love
them and train them as children of
the covenant and children of the promise.
These are the children of God.

Andrew Murray

If you want to be a teacher, remember that
you're just as likely to teach who you are
as you are to teach what you know.

Marie T. Freeman

Train your child in the way in which you
know you should have gone yourself.

C. H. Spurgeon

It is desirable that children be kind,
appreciative and pleasant. Those qualities
should be taught and not hoped for.

James Dobson

The dream begins, most of the time,
with a teacher who believes in you,
who tugs and pushes and leads you on
to the next plateau, sometimes poking you
with a sharp stick called truth.

Dan Rather

Teaching means helping the child
to realize his potential.

Erich Fromm

Good teaching is one-fourth preparation
and three-fourths pure theatre.

Gail Godwin

*Wise people's minds tell them what to say,
and that helps them be better teachers.*

Proverbs 16:23 NCV

To believe in a child is to believe in the future. Through their aspirations they will save the world. With their combined knowledge the turbulent seas of hate and injustice will be calmed. They will champion the causes of life's underdogs, forging a society without class discrimination. They will supply humanity with music and beauty as it has never known. They will endure. Towards these ends I pledge my life's work. I will supply the children with tools and knowledge to overcome the obstacles. I will pass on the wisdom of my years and temper it with patience. I shall impact in each child the desire to fulfill his or her dream. I shall teach.

Henry James

Chapter 3

A Daily Journey

*Come to Me, all you who labor and are
heavy laden, and I will give you rest.
Take My yoke upon you and learn from Me,
for I am gentle and lowly in heart,
and you will find rest for your souls.
For My yoke is easy and My burden is light.*

Matthew 11:28-30 NKJV

Even the most inspired Christian teachers can, from time to time, find themselves running on empty. The demands of daily life combined with the stresses of the classroom can drain us of our strength and rob us of the joy that is rightfully ours in Christ.

God's Word is clear: When we genuinely lift our hearts and prayers to Him, He renews our strength. Are you almost too weary to lift your head? Then bow it. Offer your concerns and your needs to your Father in heaven. He is always at your side, offering His love and His strength.

Your search to discover God's purpose for your life is not a destination; it is a journey that unfolds day by day. And, that's exactly how often you should seek direction from your Creator: one day at a time, each day followed by the next, without exception.

Are you seeking a renewed sense of purpose? Turn your heart toward God in prayer. Are you weak or worried? Take the time to delve deeply into God's Holy Word. Are you spiritually depleted? Call upon fellow believers to support you, and call upon Christ to renew your spirit and your life. When you do, you'll discover that the Creator of the universe stands always ready and always able to create a new sense of wonderment and joy in you.

———

The life of faith is a daily exploration
of the constant and countless ways in which
God's grace and love are experienced.

Eugene Peterson

Discipleship is a daily discipline:
we follow Jesus a step at a time,
a day at a time.

Warren Wiersbe

In our faith we follow in someone's steps.
In our faith we leave footprints
to guide others.
It's the principle of discipleship.

Max Lucado

Theology is an interesting school of thought. The Bible is beautiful literature. Sitting in quiet sanctuary, bathed in the amber light from stained-glass windows, having our jangled nerves soothed by the chords from an organ—all that is inspiring. But, to tell you the truth, when we leave the classroom, close the church door, and walk out into the real world, it is the indisputable proof of changed lives that makes us believers.

—

Gloria Gaither

We must live in all kinds of days, both high
days and low days, in simple dependence
upon Christ as the branch on the vine.
This is the supreme experience.

Vance Havner

Once we recognize our need for Jesus,
then the building of our faith begins.
It is a daily, moment-by-moment life
of absolute dependence upon Him
for everything.

Catherine Marshall

Make a plan now to keep a daily
appointment with God. The enemy is going
to tell you to set it aside, but you must
carve out the time. If you're too busy to
meet with the Lord, friend,
then you are simply too busy.

Charles Swindoll

Treasure Today . . .
And Use It

Time is a nonrenewable gift from God. But sometimes, we treat our time here on earth as if it were not a gift at all: We may be tempted to invest our lives in trivial pursuits and petty diversions. But our Father beckons each of us to a higher calling.

An important element of our steward-ship to God is the way that we choose to spend the time He has entrusted to us. Each waking moment holds the potential to hug a child or do a good deed or say a kind word or to offer a heartfelt prayer. Our challenge, as believers, is to use our time wisely in the service of God's work and in accordance with His plan for our lives.

Today, like every day, is a special treasure to be savored and celebrated. May we—as Christians who have so much to celebrate—never fail to praise our Creator by rejoicing in this glorious day . . . and by using it wisely.

Chapter 4

Teaching by Example

Be an example to the believers in word, in
conduct, in love, in spirit, in faith, in purity.
1 Timothy 4:12 NKJV

We teach our students by the words we speak and the lives we lead, but not necessarily in that order. Sometimes, our actions speak so loudly that they drown out our words completely. That's why, as teachers, we must make certain that the lives we lead are in harmony with the lessons we preach.

An important part of God's plan for your life is found in the example that you set for your students. Are you the kind of teacher whose life serves as a memorable model of righteousness and godliness? If so, you are a powerful force for good in your classroom and in your world.

Phillips Brooks advised, "Be such a man, and live such a life, that if every man were such as you, and every life a life like yours, this earth would be God's Paradise." And that's sound advice because our families and our students are watching . . . and so, for that matter, is God.

Example is the school of humankind,
and they will learn at no other.

Edmund Burke

Human models are more vivid
and more persuasive
than explicit moral comments.

Daniel J. Boorstin

Not only should we teach values,
but we should live them.
A sermon is better lived than preached.

J. C. Watts

I'd rather see a sermon than hear one
any day; I'd rather one should
walk with me than merely tell the way.

Edgar A. Guest

It is a great deal better to live a holy life than to talk about it. Lighthouses do not ring bells and fire cannons to call attention to their shining—they just shine.

D. L. Moody

Our walk counts far more than our talk, always!

George Mueller

Nothing speaks louder or more powerfully than a life of integrity.

Charles Swindoll

We must mirror God's love in the midst of a world full of hatred.
We are the mirrors of God's love, so we may show Jesus by our lives.

Corrie ten Boom

For one man who can introduce another to
Jesus Christ by the way he lives and by
the atmosphere of his life,
there are a thousand who can
only talk jargon about him.

Oswald Chambers

You are the light that gives light to the world . . . .
In the same way, you should be a light for other
people. Live so that they will see the good things
you do and will praise your Father in heaven.

Matthew 5:14, 16 NCV

He preaches well who lives well.
That's all the divinity I know.

Miguel de Cervantes

You can preach a better sermon
with your life than with your lips.

Oliver Goldsmith

Children have more need of
models than critics.

Joseph Joubert

Your Speech

Your life is a sermon. What kind of
sermon will you preach? The words you
choose to speak may have some impact on
others, but not nearly as much impact as
the life you choose to live. Today, pause
to consider the tone, the theme, and the
context of your particular sermon, and ask
yourself if it's a message that you're proud to
deliver.

Chapter 5

Greatness Through Service

Be devoted to one another in brotherly love.
Honor one another above yourselves.
Romans 12:10 NIV

As a teacher, you have chosen a life of service. Congratulations. Jesus teaches that the most esteemed men and women are not the political leaders or the captains of industry. To the contrary, Jesus teaches that the greatest among us are those who choose to minister and to serve.

When you decided to become a teacher, you demonstrated your willingness to serve in a very tangible way. As a result, you can be comforted by the knowledge that your kindness and generosity will touch the lives of students in ways that you may never fully comprehend. But God knows the impact of your good works, and He will bless you because of them.

The words of Galatians 6:9 are clear: "Let us not become weary in doing good, for at the proper time we will reap a harvest if we do not give up" (NIV). May you never grow weary of your role as a teacher, and may your good works continue to bless your students long after the final school bell has rung.

We are only fully alive when
we're helping others.

Rick Warren

Holy service in constant fellowship
with God is heaven below.

C. H. Spurgeon

Employ whatever God has entrusted you
with, in doing good, all possible good,
in every possible kind and degree.

John Wesley

Without God, we cannot.
Without us, God will not.

St. Augustine

Carve your name on hearts, not on marble.

C. H. Spurgeon

That's what I love about serving God.
In His eyes, there are no little people . . .
because there are no big people.
We are all on the same playing field.

Joni Eareckson Tada

Have thy tools ready;
God will find thee work.

Charles Kingsley

Happiness consists in giving
and in serving others.

Henry Drummond

*Each of you should look not only
to your own interests,
but also to the interest of others.*

Philippians 2:4 NIV

Chapter 6

The Power of Purpose

*I can do all things through Christ
which strengtheneth me.*
Philippians 4:13 KJV

I f you're a teacher with too many obliga-
tions and too few hours in which to
meet them, you are not alone: yours is a
demanding profession. As a dedicated teacher, you may experience moments when you
feel overworked, overstressed, and under-
appreciated. Thankfully, God stands ready
to renew your optimism and your strength if
you turn to Him.

As a teacher, you are helping to shape
the lives of your students. Your work is
profoundly important. Consider it God's
work.

When you feel worried or weary,
focus your thoughts upon God and upon
His plans for you. Then, ask Him for the
wisdom to prioritize your life. Finally, ask
God for the strength and courage to fulfill
your responsibilities.

When you sincerely seek to follow God's
path for your life, you will become energized.
And then, with God as your partner, you'll
be amazed at the things that the two of you
can accomplish.

It's incredible to realize that
what we do each day has meaning
in the big picture of God's plan.

Bill Hybels

Aim at Heaven and you will get
earth "thrown in";
aim at earth and you will get neither.

C. S. Lewis

We must focus on prayer as the main thrust
to accomplish God's will and purpose
on earth. The forces against us have never
been greater, and this is the only way we can
release God's power to become victorious.

John Maxwell

Without God, life has no purpose,
and without purpose, life has no meaning.

Rick Warren

If the Lord calls you, He will equip you
for the task He wants you to fulfill.

Warren Wiersbe

For God hath not given us the spirit of fear;
but of power, and of love, and of a sound mind.

2 Timothy 1:7 KJV

A Prayer

Lord, sometimes life is difficult. Sometimes,
I am worried, weary, or discouraged.
The classroom can be a struggle, but,
when I lift my eyes to You, Father,
You strengthen me. Today, I will turn
to You, Lord, for strength,
for hope, and for salvation.
Amen

Chapter 7

Faith for the Future

*"I say this because I know what I am
planning for you,"* says the Lord.
*"I have good plans for you, not plans to hurt you.
I will give you hope and a good future."*
Jeremiah 29:11 NCV

As you consider God's unfolding plans for your life, you will undoubtedly look to the future . . . after all, the future is where those plans will take place. But sometimes, the future may seem foreboding indeed.

In these uncertain times, it's easy to lose faith in the possibility of a better tomorrow . . . but it's wrong. God instructs us to trust His wisdom, His plan, and His love. When we do so, the future becomes a glorious opportunity to help others, to praise our Creator, and to share God's Good News.

Do you have faith in the ultimate goodness of God's plan? You should. And, do you have faith in the abundant opportunities that await your students? Hopefully, you do. After all, the confidence that you display in your students can be contagious: your belief in them can have a profound impact on the way they view themselves and their world.

Today, as you stand before your classroom, help your students face the future with optimism, hope, and self-confidence. After all, even in these uncertain times, God still has the last word. And His love endures to all generations, including this one.

The future lies all before us. Shall it only be
a slight advance upon what we usually do?
Ought it not to be a bound,
a leap forward to altitudes of endeavor
and success undreamed of before?

Annie Armstrong

Take courage.
We walk in the wilderness today
and in the Promised Land tomorrow.

D. L. Moody

Do not limit the limitless God!
With Him, face the future unafraid
because you are never alone.

Mrs. Charles E. Cowman

What joy that the Bible tells us the great
comfort that the best is yet to be.
Our outlook goes beyond this world.

Corrie ten Boom

You can look forward with hope,
because one day there will be
no more separation, no more scars,
and no more suffering
in My Father's House.
It's the home of your dreams!

Anne Graham Lotz

Every experience God gives us,
every person he brings into our lives,
is the perfect preparation for the future
that only he can see.

Corrie ten Boom

The future starts today, not tomorrow.

Pope John Paul II

Chapter 8

Renewal, Perspective, and Purpose

Create in me a clean heart, O God;
and renew a right spirit within me.
Psalm 51:10 KJV

For most of us, life is busy and complicated. And, as teachers, we have countless responsibilities that begin long before the school bell rings and end long after the last student has left the classroom. Amid the rush and crush of the daily grind, it is easy to lose perspective . . . easy, but wrong. When our world seems to be spinning out of control, we must simply seek to regain perspective by slowing ourselves down and then turning our thoughts and prayers toward God.

Do you carve out quiet moments each day to offer thanksgiving and praise to your Creator? You should. During these moments of stillness, you will often sense the love and wisdom of our Lord.

The familiar words of Psalm 46:10 remind us to "Be still, and know that I am God" (KJV). When we do so, we encounter the awesome presence of our loving Heavenly Father, and we are blessed beyond words. But, when we ignore the presence of our Creator, we rob ourselves of His perspective, His peace, and His joy.

Today and every day, carve out a time to be still before God. When you do, you

can face the day's complications with
the wisdom and power that only He can
provide.

———

If the pace and the push, the noise
and the crowds are getting to you,
it's time to stop the nonsense and find
a place of solace to refresh your spirit.

Charles Swindoll

Like a spring of pure water,
God's peace in our hearts brings cleansing
and refreshment to our minds and bodies.

Billy Graham

He is the God of wholeness and restoration.

Stormie Omartian

When you and I hurt deeply, what we really
need is not an explanation from God
but a revelation of God. We need to see how
great God is; we need to recover our lost
perspective on life. Things get out of
proportion when we are suffering,
and it takes a vision of something
bigger than ourselves to get
life's dimensions adjusted again.

Warren Wiersbe

Repentance removes old sins and wrong
attitudes, and it opens the way for
the Holy Spirit to restore our spiritual
health.

Shirley Dobson

*And do not be conformed to this world,
but be transformed by the renewing of your mind,
that you may prove what is that good
and acceptable and perfect will of God.*

Romans 12:2 NKJV

Chapter 9

Encouraging
Our Students

*Let's see how inventive we can be
in encouraging love and helping out . . .
spurring each other on.*
Hebrews 10:24-25 MSG

Life is a team sport, and all of us need occasional pats on the back from our teammates and our coaches. Great teachers, like great coaches, inspire their students to learn, to work, to grow, and to persevere.

Never has the need been greater for teachers who understand the art of encouragement. This world can be a difficult place, and countless students may be troubled by the challenges of everyday life. Our task, as teachers, is to become beacons of encouragement inside the classroom and out.

The 118th Psalm reminds us, "This is the day which the Lord hath made; we will rejoice and be glad in it" (v. 24 KJV). As we rejoice in this day that the Lord has given us, let us remember that an important part of today's celebration is the time we spend celebrating others. Each day provides countless opportunities to encourage other people and to praise their good works. When we do, we not only spread seeds of joy and happiness, we also follow the commandments of God's Holy Word.

Today, look for the good in others and celebrate the good that you find. Who knows? Your encouraging words might just change someone's day . . . or someone's life.

————

A lot of people have gone further than they thought they could because someone else thought they could.

Zig Ziglar

God is still in the process of dispensing gifts, and He uses ordinary individuals like us to develop those gifts in other people.

Howard Hendricks

People who inspire others are those who see invisible bridges at the end of dead-end streets.

Charles Swindoll

Encouragement is the oxygen of the soul.

John Maxwell

Talk happiness.
The world is sad enough without your woe.

Ella Wheeler Wilcox

Words. Do you fully understand their
power? Can any of us really grasp
the mighty force behind the things we say?
Do we stop and think before
we speak, considering the potency
of the words we utter?

Joni Eareckson Tada

When you talk, choose the very same words
that you would use if Jesus were looking
over your shoulder. Because He is.

Marie T. Freeman

The biggest disease today is not leprosy
or tuberculosis, but rather the feeling
of being unwanted.

Mother Teresa

Never take away hope from
any human being.

Oliver Wendell Holmes, Sr.

For every one of us who succeeds,
it's because there's somebody
there to show us the way.

Oprah Winfrey

*Kind words are like honey—
sweet to the soul and healthy for the body.*

Proverbs 16:24 NLT

Correction does much, but encouragement
does more. Encouragement after censure
is as the sun after a shower.

Goethe

Invest in the human soul.
Who knows, it might be a diamond
in the rough.

Mary McLeod Bethune

When someone does something good,
applaud!
You'll make two people feel good.

Sam Goldwyn

———

**Encouragement is contagious.
You can't lift other people up
without lifting yourself up, too.**

Chapter 10

Praying *on* Purpose *for* Purpose

*The intense prayer of the righteous
is very powerful.*
James 5:16 HCSB

"The power of prayer": these words are so familiar, yet sometimes we forget what they mean. Prayer is a powerful tool for communicating with our Creator; it is an opportunity to commune with the Giver of all things good. Prayer is not a thing to be taken lightly or to be used infrequently.

All too often, amid the rush of daily life, we may lose sight of God's presence in our lives. Instead of turning to Him for guidance and for comfort, we depend, instead, upon our own resources. To do so is a profound mistake. Prayer should never be reserved for mealtimes or for bedtimes; it should be an ever-present focus in our daily lives.

In his first letter to the Thessalonians, Paul wrote, "Rejoice evermore. Pray without ceasing. In every thing give thanks: for this is the will of God in Christ Jesus concerning you" (5:17-18 KJV). Paul's words apply to every Christian of every generation.

Do you have questions you can't answer? Are you genuinely seeking to understand God's plan for your life? If so, then turn your concerns over to Him—quietly, prayerfully, earnestly, and often. Then listen for His answers . . . and trust the answers that He gives. Instead of turning things over in your mind, turn them over to God in prayer. He is most certainly listening, and He wants to hear from you now. You, in turn, most certainly *need* to hear from Him. Now.

————

Prayer guards hearts and minds and causes God to bring peace out of chaos.

Beth Moore

On our knees we are the most powerful force on earth.

Billy Graham

He that is never on his knees on earth, shall never stand upon his feet in heaven.

C. H. Spurgeon

The purpose of all prayer is to find
God's will and to make that will our prayer.

Catherine Marshall

We must focus on prayer as the main thrust
to accomplish God's will and purpose on
earth. The forces against us have never been
greater, and this is the only way we can
release God's power to become victorious.

John Maxwell

Leadership requires vision, and whence
will vision come except from hours spent
in the presence of God in humble
and fervent prayer?

A. W. Tozer

*Be kindly affectionate to one another with
brotherly love, in honor giving preference to one
another; not lagging in diligence, fervent in spirit,
serving the Lord; rejoicing in hope, patient in
tribulation, continuing steadfastly in prayer.*

Romans 12:10–12 NKJV

Only God can move mountains,
but faith and prayer can move God.

E. M. Bounds

The Christian prays in every situation,
in his walks for recreation,
in his dealing with others, in silence,
in reading, in all rational pursuits.

Clement of Alexandria

Don't pray when you feel like it;
make an appointment
with the King and keep it.

Corrie ten Boom

Prayer succeeds when all else fails.

E. M. Bounds

Sometimes, the Answer Is "No"

God does not answer all of our prayers in the affirmative, nor should He. His job is not to grant all our earthly requests; His job is to offer us eternal salvation (for which we must be eternally grateful).

When we are disappointed by the realities of life-here-on-earth, we should remember that our prayers are always answered by a sovereign, all-knowing God, and that we must trust Him, whether He answers "Yes," "No," or "Not yet."

Chapter 11

The Faith to Move Mountains

*I tell you the truth, if you have faith
and do not doubt . . .
you can say to this mountain
"Go and throw yourself into the sea,"
and it will be done.*
Matthew 21:21 NIV

As a dedicated member of the teaching profession, you have mountains to climb *and* mountains to move. Jesus taught His disciples that if they had faith, they could move mountains. You can too. When you place your faith, your trust, indeed your life in the hands of Christ Jesus, you'll be amazed at the marvelous things He can do.

When a suffering woman sought healing by simply touching the hem of His garment, Jesus turned and said, "Daughter, be of good comfort; thy faith hath made thee whole" (Matthew 9:22 KJV). We, too, can be made whole when we place our faith completely and unwaveringly in the person of Jesus Christ.

Concentration camp survivor Corrie ten Boom relied on faith during her months of imprisonment and torture. Later, despite the fact that four of her family members had died in Nazi death camps, Corrie's faith was unshaken. She wrote, "There is no pit so deep that God's love is not deeper still." Christian teachers take note: Genuine faith in God means faith in all circumstances, happy or sad, joyful or tragic.

If, today, your faith is being tested, know that your Savior is near. If you reach out to Him in faith, He will give you peace, perspective, and hope. If you are content to touch even the smallest fragment of the Master's garment, He will make you whole.

———

Faith is a living, daring confidence in God's grace, so sure and certain that a man would stake his life on it a thousand times.

Martin Luther

Faith is like an empty, open hand stretched out towards God, with nothing to offer and everything to receive.

John Calvin

Our faith becomes stronger as we express it;
a growing faith is a sharing faith.

Billy Graham

The Christian life is one of faith,
where we find ourselves routinely
overdriving our headlights but knowing
it's okay because God is in control
and has a purpose behind it.

Bill Hybels

We must trust as if it all depended on
God and work as if it all depended on us.

C. H. Spurgeon

I do not want merely to possess a faith;
I want a faith that possesses me.

Charles Kingsley

Let me encourage you to continue to wait
with faith. God may not perform a miracle,
but He is trustworthy to touch you
and make you whole where there
used to be a hole.

Lisa Whelchel

Faith is not merely you holding on to
God—it is God holding on to you.

E. Stanley Jones

*I tell you the truth, if you have faith
as small as a mustard seed, you can say
to this mountain, "Move from here to there"
and it will move. Nothing will be
impossible for you.*

Matthew 17:20 NIV

God's Timing?
It's Worth the Wait

Are you anxious for God to work out His plan for your life? Who isn't? As believers, we all want God to do great things for us and through us, and we want Him to do those things now. But sometimes, God has other plans. Sometimes, God's timetable does not coincide with our own. It's worth noting, however, that God's timetable is always perfect.

The next time you find your patience tested to the limit, remember that the world unfolds according to God's plan, not ours. Sometimes, we must wait patiently, and that's as it should be. After all, think how patient God has been with us.

Chapter 12

Sharing
God's Wisdom

If any of you lacks wisdom, he should ask God,
who gives generously to all without finding fault,
and it will be given to him.
James 1:5 NIV

Do you seek wisdom for yourself and for your students? Of course you do. But as a savvy teacher, you know that wisdom can be an elusive commodity in today's world. We live in a society filled with temptations and distractions; it's easy for teachers and students to lose sight of the ultimate wisdom. The ultimate source of wisdom, of course, is the Word of God.

When you begin a daily study of God's Word and live according to His commandments, you will become wise . . . and so, in time, will many of your students. But if you expect a blanket of maturity to settle quietly across the entirety of your classroom, you'll be disappointed. Wisdom is not like a mushroom; it does not spring up overnight. It is, instead, like an oak tree that starts as a tiny acorn, grows into a sapling, and eventually reaches up to the sky, tall and strong.

When you study God's Word and live according to His commandments, you will become a wise teacher . . . and you will be a blessing to your friends, to your family, to your students, and to the world.

Do you want to be wise?
Choose wise friends.

Charles Swindoll

There are some things that can be learned
by the head, but Christ crucified
can only be learned by the heart.

C. H. Spurgeon

Knowledge can be found in books or in
school. Wisdom, on the other hand,
starts with God . . . and ends there.

Marie T. Freeman

The images of men's wits and knowledge
remain in books. They generate still,
and cast their seeds in the minds of others,
provoking and causing infinite actions
and opinions in succeeding ages.

Francis Bacon

Wisdom is knowledge applied.
Head knowledge is useless on the battlefield.
Knowledge stamped on the heart
makes one wise.

Beth Moore

God does not give His counsel to
the curious or the careless;
He reveals His will to the concerned
and to the consecrated.

Warren Wiersbe

The man who prays ceases to be a fool.

Oswald Chambers

The essence of wisdom, from a practical
standpoint, is pausing long enough to look
at our lives—invitations, opportunities,
relationships—from God's perspective.
And then acting on it.

Charles Stanley

Most of us go through life praying a little,
planning a little, jockeying for position,
hoping but never being quite certain of
anything, and always secretly afraid that we
will miss the way. This is a tragic waste of
truth and never gives rest to the heart.
There is a better way. It is to repudiate
our own wisdom and take instead
the infinite wisdom of God.

A. W. Tozer

The fruit of wisdom is Christlikeness,
peace, humility, and love.
And, the root of it is faith in Christ
as the manifested wisdom of God.

J. I. Packer

*Let the word of Christ dwell in you richly
in all wisdom; teaching and admonishing one
another in psalms and hymns
and spiritual songs, singing with grace
in your hearts to the Lord.*

Colossians 3:16 KJV

Focus on Purposes, Not Wishes

As you consider God's plan and purpose for you and your family, ask yourself this question: "Is this *my* wish list or God's?" If you're struggling mightily to keep up with the Joneses, you may be struggling in vain. But if you set your personal wish list aside and instead seek God's purposes for your life, He will lead you in the direction you should go. Never allow greed, fear, selfishness, or pride to separate you from the will of God. Seek His kingdom first, and then have faith that He will provide all the things that you *need*, even if He does not grant all the things that you *want*.

Chapter 13

The Power
of Optimism

*My cup runs over. Surely goodness
and mercy shall follow me all the days of my life;
and I will dwell in the house of the Lord Forever.*

Psalm 23:5-6 NKJV

Christians have every reason to be optimistic about life. As Billy Graham observed, "Christ can put a spring in your step and a thrill in your heart. Optimism and cheerfulness are products of knowing Christ." But sometimes, when we are tired or frustrated, optimism and cheerfulness seem like distant promises. They are not. Thankfully, our God stands ready to restore us: "I will give you a new heart and put a new spirit in you . . ." (Ezekiel 36:26 NIV). Our task, of course, is to let Him.

Today, accept the new spirit that God seeks to infuse into your heart. Think optimistically about yourself, your students, your school, and your world. Rejoice in this glorious day that the Lord has given you, and share your optimism with your friends, with your coworkers, and with your students. Your enthusiasm will be contagious. And your words will bring healing and comfort to a world that needs both.

The essence of optimism is that it takes
no account of the present, but it is a source
of inspiration, of vitality, and of hope.
Where others have resigned, it enables
a man to hold his head high, to claim
the future for himself,
and not abandon it to his enemy.

Dietrich Bonhoeffer

Make the least of all that goes and
the most of all that comes. Don't regret
what is past. Cherish what you have.
Look forward to all that is to come.
And most important of all, rely moment
by moment on Jesus Christ.

Gigi Graham Tchividjian

The people whom I have seen succeed
best in life have always been cheerful
and hopeful people who went about their
business with a smile on their faces.

Charles Kingsley

Those who are God's without reserve are,
in every sense, content.

Hannah Whitall Smith

Keep your feet on the ground,
but let your heart soar as high as it will.
Refuse to be average or to surrender to
the chill of your spiritual environment.

A. W. Tozer

The Christian should be
an alleluia from head to foot!

St. Augustine

Never yield to gloomy anticipation.
Place your hope and confidence in God.
He has no record of failure.

Mrs. Charles E. Cowman

We are all faced with a series of great opportunities, brilliantly disguised as unsolvable problems. Unsolvable without God's wisdom, that is.

Charles Swindoll

Worry is the senseless process of cluttering up tomorrow's opportunities with leftover problems from today.

Barbara Johnson

Do not build up obstacles in your imagination. Difficulties must be studied and dealt with, but they must not be magnified by fear.

Norman Vincent Peale

Make me hear joy and gladness.

Psalm 51:8 NKJV

Be a Realistic Optimist

Your attitude toward the future will help create your future. So think realistically about yourself, your family, and your situation while making a conscious effort to focus on hopes, not fears. When you do, you'll put the self-fulfilling prophecy to work *for you and yours.*

Chapter 14

Stillness Before God

Be still, and know that I am God.
Psalm 46:10 KJV

Are you so busy that you rush through the day with scarcely a single moment for quiet contemplation and prayer? If so, it's time to slow down and reorder your priorities.

We live in a noisy world, a world filled with distractions, frustrations, and complications. But if we allow the distractions of the world—or the distractions of a clamorous classroom—to separate us from God's peace and God's purposes, we do ourselves a disservice.

If we are to discover God's unfolding purpose for our lives, we must take time each day for prayer and for meditation. We must make ourselves still in the presence of our Creator. We must quiet our minds and our hearts so that we might sense God's will, God's love, and God's Son.

Has the busy pace of life robbed you of the peace that might otherwise be yours through Jesus Christ? Nothing is more important than the time you spend with your Savior. So be still and claim the inner peace that is your spiritual birthright: the peace of Jesus Christ. It is offered freely; it has been paid for in full; it is yours for the asking. So ask. And then share.

The manifold rewards of a serious,
consistent prayer life demonstrate clearly
that time with our Lord
should be our first priority.

Shirley Dobson

In the center of a hurricane there is
absolute quiet and peace.
There is no safer place than
in the center of the will of God.

Corrie ten Boom

We Christians must simplify our lives
or lose untold treasures on earth and in
eternity. Modern civilization is so complex
as to make the devotional life all
but impossible. The need for solitude
and quietness was never greater
than it is today.

A. W. Tozer

Are you weak? Weary? Confused? Troubled?
Pressured? How is your relationship with
God? Is it held in its place of priority?
I believe the greater the pressure,
the greater your need for
time alone with Him.

Kay Arthur

Speed-reading may be a good thing,
but it was never meant for the Bible.
It takes calm, thoughtful, prayerful
meditation on the Word to extract
its deepest nourishment.

Vance Havner

Let this be your chief object in prayer,
to realize the presence of your
heavenly Father. Let your watchword be:
Alone with God.

Andrew Murray

The remedy for distractions
is the same now as it was in earlier
and simpler times: prayer, meditation,
and the cultivation of the inner life.

A. W. Tozer

The world is full of noise.
Might we not set ourselves to learn
silence, stillness, solitude?

Elisabeth Elliot

God is the friend of silence.
See how nature—trees, flowers, grass—grows
in silence; see the stars, the moon and
the sun, how they move in silence.
We need silence to be able to touch souls.

Mother Teresa

I wait quietly before God, for my hope is in him.

Psalm 62:5 NLT

Turn Down the Noise, Turn Up Your Thoughts

So much noise and so little time! In today's world, we are bombarded with instant messages, ubiquitous communications, blaring music, and unlimited information. Perhaps you've allowed this noise to fill every waking moment of your life. If so, it's time to click off the radio, the television, the computer, and the cell phone—for awhile.

Try this experiment: the next time you're driving alone in your automobile, do so without radio, CDs, or cell phones. And then, have a quiet talk with God about His plans for your life. You may be surprised to discover that sometimes the most important answers are the ones you receive in silence.

Chapter 15

The Power of Perseverance

Thanks be to God! He gives us the victory
through our Lord Jesus Christ.
Therefore, my dear brothers, stand firm.
Let nothing move you. Always give yourselves
fully to the work of the Lord, because you know
that your labor in the Lord is not in vain.
1 Corinthians 15:57-58 NIV

The familiar saying is true: "Life is a marathon, not a sprint." And, the same can be said of the teaching profession. Teaching requires determination, especially on those difficult days when the students are in an uproar and the lesson plan is in disarray.

In a world filled with roadblocks and stumbling blocks, we need strength, courage, and perseverance. And, as an example of perfect perseverance, we need look no further than our Savior, Jesus Christ. Our Savior finished what He began, and so must we.

Perhaps you are in a hurry for God to reveal His unfolding plans for your life. If so, be forewarned: God operates on His own timetable, not yours. Sometimes, God may answer your prayers with silence, and when He does, you must patiently persevere. In times of trouble, you must remain steadfast and trust in the merciful goodness of your Heavenly Father. Whatever your challenge, God can handle it. Your job is to keep persevering until He does.

Jesus taught that perseverance
is the essential element in prayer.

E. M. Bounds

In the Bible, patience is not a passive
acceptance of circumstances.
It is a courageous perseverance
in the face of suffering and difficulty.

Warren Wiersbe

Your life is not a boring stretch of highway.
It's a straight line to heaven. And just look
at the fields ripening along the way.
Look at the tenacity and endurance.
Look at the grains of righteousness.
You'll have quite a crop at harvest . . .
so don't give up!

Joni Eareckson Tada

All rising to a great place
is by a winding stair.

Francis Bacon

Every achievement worth remembering is
stained with the blood of diligence and
scarred by the wounds of disappointment.

Charles Swindoll

Only the man who follows the command
of Jesus single-mindedly and unresistingly
lets his yoke rest upon him, finds his burden
easy, and under its gentle pressure receives
the power to persevere in the right way.

Dietrich Bonhoeffer

By perseverance, the snail reached the ark.

C. H. Spurgeon

Let us not become weary in doing good,
for at the proper time we will reap
a harvest if we do not give up.

Galatians 6:9 NIV

Chapter 16

Purposeful
Leadership

*Those who are wise will shine like
the brightness of the heavens,
and those who lead many to righteousness,
like the stars for ever and ever.*
Daniel 12:3 NIV

As a teacher, you are automatically placed in a position of leadership. Unless, you assume firm control over your students, effective learning will not take place in your classroom.

John Maxwell writes, "Great leaders understand that the right attitude will set the right atmosphere, which enables the right response from others." As the leader of your class, it's up to you to set the proper balance between discipline and amusement, between entertainment and scholarship.

Savvy teachers learn to strike an appropriate balance between discipline (which is necessary for maintaining order) and fun (which is necessary for maintaining interest). The rest, of course, is up to the students.

Are you the kind of teacher whose class you would want to attend if *you* were a student? Hopefully so, because our world always needs another competent, Christ-centered leader . . . and so, for that matter, do your students.

When God wants to accomplish something,
He calls dedicated men and women
to challenge His people and lead the way.

Warren Wiersbe

No one deserves the right to lead
without first persevering through pain
and heartache and failure.

Charles Swindoll

Great leaders understand that the right
attitude will set the right atmosphere, which
enables the right response from others.

John Maxwell

When we read of the great Biblical leaders,
we see that it was not uncommon for
God to ask them to wait,
not just a day or two, but for years,
until God was ready for them to act.

Gloria Gaither

Leadership requires vision, and whence
will vision come except from hours spent
in the presence of God in
humble and fervent prayer?

A. W. Tozer

Whenever I meet someone, I try to imagine
him wearing an invisible sign saying,
"Make me feel important!" I respond to
the sign immediately, and it works.

Mary Kay Ash

Effective leadership is putting
first things first. Effective management is
discipline, carrying it out.

Stephen Covey

*His lord said unto him, Well done, thou good
and faithful servant: thou hast been faithful over
a few things, I will make thee ruler over many
things: enter thou into the joy of thy lord.*

Matthew 25:21 KJV

Chapter 17

Asking God

Whatever you ask for in prayer,
believe that you have received it,
and it will be yours.
Mark 11:24 NIV

Have you fervently asked God for guidance or for strength? If so, then you're continually inviting your Creator to reveal Himself in a variety of ways. As a follower of Christ, you must do no less.

Jesus made it clear to His disciples: they should petition God to meet their needs. So should we. Genuine, heartfelt prayer produces powerful changes in us and in our world. When we lift our hearts to God, we open ourselves to a never-ending source of divine wisdom and infinite love.

Do you have questions about your future that you simply can't answer? Do you have needs that you simply can't meet by yourself? Do you sincerely seek to know God's purpose for your life inside the classroom and outside it? If so, ask Him for direction, for protection, and for strength—and then keep asking Him every day that you live. Whatever your need, no matter how great or small, pray about it and never lose hope. God is not just near; He is here, and He's perfectly capable of answering your prayers. Now, it's up to you to ask.

God uses our most stumbling, faltering
faith-steps as the open door to His doing
for us "more than we ask or think."

Catherine Marshall

When you ask God to do something,
don't ask timidly;
put your whole heart into it.

Marie T. Freeman

God makes prayer as easy as possible for us.
He's completely approachable and available,
and He'll never mock or upbraid us for
bringing our needs before Him.

Shirley Dobson

If we do not have hearts that call out to him,
we forfeit the deliverance. "You do not have,
because you do not ask God"
(James 4:2 NIV) is probably the saddest
commentary on any life,
especially the life of a Christian.

Jim Cymbala

Some people think God does not like to be
troubled with our constant asking.
But, the way to trouble God
is not to come at all.

D. L. Moody

God will help us become the people we are
meant to be, if only we will ask Him.

Hannah Whitall Smith

We honor God by asking for great things
when they are a part of His promise.
We dishonor Him and cheat ourselves when
we ask for molehills where
He has promised mountains.

Vance Havner

Ask and it shall be given to you;
seek and you shall find; knock and it shall be
opened to you. For every one who asks receives,
and he who seeks finds,
and to him who knocks it shall be opened.

Matthew 7:7-8 NASB

Chapter 18

Teaching Discipline

The fear of the Lord is the beginning
of knowledge, but fools despise
wisdom and discipline.
Proverbs 1:7 NIV

As a teacher, you are charged with a thankless task: controlling students who would prefer not to be controlled. Hopefully, your students will learn that disciplined behavior is a prerequisite for success both inside *and* outside the classroom.

Those who study the Bible are confronted again and again with God's intention that His children (of all ages) lead disciplined lives. God doesn't reward laziness or misbehavior. To the contrary, He expects His own to adopt a disciplined approach to their lives, and He punishes those who disobey His commandments.

Do you teach the importance of discipline? If so, many of your students are learning powerful, life-changing lessons about the rewards of a disciplined lifestyle. And rest assured that your example will speak far more loudly than your lectures. So teach the fine art of responsible behavior through your words and your actions, but not necessarily in that order.

Talking in class disturbs the teacher and
the class. The habit of self-control is
not easily acquired, but when the pupil has
his tongue under control, as, St. James says,
"He is able to bridle the whole body."

Fanny Jackson Coppin

Discipline of the school should proceed
from the life of the school as a whole and
not directly from the teacher.

John Dewey

If one examines the secret behind
a championship football team,
a magnificent orchestra, or a successful
business, the principal ingredient
is invariably discipline.

James Dobson

The alternative to discipline is disaster.

Vance Havner

The secret of a happy life is to delight in
duty. When duty becomes delight,
then burdens become blessings.

Warren Wiersbe

The effective Christians of history
have been men and women of great
personal discipline—mental discipline,
discipline of the body, discipline of
the tongue, and discipline of the emotion.

Billy Graham

True willpower and courage are not only
on the battlefield, but also in
everyday conquests over our inertia,
laziness, and boredom.

D. L. Moody

Apply your heart to discipline
And your ears to words of knowledge.

Proverbs 23:12 NASB

Chapter 19

On a Personal Mission for God

Now then we are ambassadors for Christ . . . .
2 Corinthians 5:20 KJV

Whether you realize it or not, you are on a personal mission for God. As a Christian teacher, that mission is straightforward: Honor your Creator, accept Christ as your Savior, teach your students truth, and serve those who cross your path.

Of course, you will encounter impediments as you attempt to discover the *exact* nature of God's purpose for your life, but you must never lose sight of the *overriding* purposes that God has established for all believers through the revelations of His Holy Word. When you apply God's commandments to every aspect of your life, you will earn countless blessings for yourself, your family, and your students.

Every day offers fresh opportunities to serve God, to worship Him, and to seek His will. When you do, He will bless you in miraculous ways. May you continue to seek God's purposes, may you trust His Word, and may you place Him where He belongs: at the very center of your life.

The one supreme business of life is to find
God's plan for your life and live it.

E. Stanley Jones

God wants to use us
as He used His own Son.

Oswald Chambers

Nothing happens by happenstance.
I am not in the hands of fate, nor am I the
victim of man's whims or the devil's ploys.
There is One who sits above man,
above Satan, and above all heavenly hosts
as the ultimate authority of all the universe.
That One is my God and my Father!

Kay Arthur

God's grand strategy, birthed in his grace
toward us in Christ, and nurtured through
the obedience of disciplined faith,
is to release us into the redeemed life of our
heart, knowing it will lead us back to him
even as the North Star guides a ship across
the vast unknown surface of the ocean.

John Eldredge

Missions is God finding those
whose hearts are right with Him
and placing them where they can make
a difference for His kingdom.

Henry Blackaby

How many people have you made
homesick for God?

Oswald Chambers

God is preparing you as his chosen arrow.
As yet your shaft is hidden in his quiver,
in the shadows, but, at the precise moment,
he will reach for you and launch you
to that place of his appointment.

Charles Swindoll

*You are the light of the world. A city on a hill
cannot be hidden. Neither do people light a lamp
and put it under a bowl. Instead they put it
on its stand, and it gives light to everyone
in the house. In the same way, let your light
shine before men, that they may see your good
deeds and praise your Father in heaven.*

Matthew 5:14-16 NIV

Chapter 20

Worship and Praise
with a Purpose

But the hour is coming, and now is,
when the true worshipers will worship the Father
in spirit and truth; for the Father is seeking such
to worship Him. God is Spirit, and those who
worship Him must worship in spirit and truth.
John 4:23-24 NKJV

All of mankind is engaged in the practice of worship. Some choose to worship God and, as a result, reap the joy that He intends for His children. Others distance themselves from God by worshiping such things as earthly possessions or personal gratification . . . and when they do so, they suffer.

Today, as one way of worshipping God, make every aspect of your life a cause for celebration and praise. Praise God for the blessings and opportunities that He has given you, and live according to the beautiful words found in the 5th chapter of 1 Thessalonians: "Rejoice evermore. Pray without ceasing. In every thing give thanks: for this is the will of God in Christ Jesus concerning you" (vv. 16-18 KJV).

God deserves your worship, your prayers, your praise, and your thanks. And you deserve the joy that is yours when you worship Him with your prayers, with your deeds, and with your life.

Praise is the highest occupation
of any being.

Max Lucado

A man can no more diminish God's glory
by refusing to worship Him than a lunatic
can put out the sun by scribbling the word
darkness on the walls of his cell.

C. S. Lewis

The fact that we were created to enjoy God
and to worship him forever is
etched upon our souls.

Jim Cymbala

When you use your life for God's glory,
everything you do can become
an act of worship.

Rick Warren

It is impossible to worship God
and remain unchanged.

Henry Blackaby

Worship is an act which develops feelings
for God, not a feeling for God which is
expressed in an act of worship. When we
obey the command to praise God
in worship, our deep, essential need to be
in relationship with God is nurtured.

Eugene Peterson

The time for universal praise is sure
to come some day.
Let us begin to do our part now.

Hannah Whitall Smith

I will praise the Lord at all times,
I will constantly speak his praises.

Psalm 34:1 NLT

Chapter 21

A Lifetime of Spiritual Growth

*But grow in the grace and knowledge of our Lord
and Savior Jesus Christ. To Him be the glory,
both now and to the day of eternity.*
2 Peter 3:18 NASB

The journey toward spiritual maturity lasts a lifetime: As Christian teachers, we can and should continue to grow in the love and the knowledge of our Savior as long as we live. When we cease to grow, either emotionally or spiritually, we do ourselves, our families, and our students a profound disservice. But, if we study God's Word, if we obey His commandments, and if we live in the center of His will, we will not be "stagnant" believers; we will, instead, be growing Christians . . . and that's exactly what God wants for our lives.

Many of life's most important lessons are painful to learn, but spiritual growth need not take place only in times of adversity. We must seek to grow in our knowledge and love of the Lord in every season of life. Thankfully, God always stands at the door; whenever we are ready to reach out to Him, He will answer.

In those quiet moments when we open our hearts to God, the One who made us keeps remaking us. He gives us direction, perspective, wisdom, and courage. And, the appropriate moment to accept those spiritual gifts is always the present one.

Our vision is so limited we can hardly
imagine a love that does not show itself in
protection from suffering. The love of God
did not protect His own Son. He will not
necessarily protect us—not from anything
it takes to make us like His Son.
A lot of hammering and chiseling
and purifying by fire will
have to go into the process.

Elisabeth Elliot

The vigor of our spiritual lives will be in
exact proportion to the place held by
the Bible in our lives and in our thoughts.

George Mueller

Keep your face upturned to Christ
as the flowers do to the sun.
Look, and your soul shall live and grow.

Hannah Whitall Smith

We should not be upset when unexpected
and upsetting things happen.
God, in His wisdom, means to make
something of us which we have not yet
attained, and He is dealing
with us accordingly.

J. I. Packer

A Christian is never in a state of completion
but always in the process of becoming.

Martin Luther

Enjoy the adventure of receiving God
guidance. Taste it, revel in it, appreciate
the fact that the journey is often a lot more
exciting than arriving at the destination.

Bill Hybels

*Long for the pure milk of the word,
so that by it you may grow in respect to salvation.*

1 Peter 2:2 NASB

Chapter 22

At Peace
with Your Purpose

*The peace of God, which surpasses
all understanding, will guard your hearts
and minds through Christ Jesus.*
Philippians 4:7 NKJV

As every teacher knows, peace can be a scarce commodity in a demanding, 21st-century classroom. How, then, can we find the peace that we so desperately desire? By turning our days and our lives over to God.

The beautiful words of John 14:27 give us hope: "Peace I leave with you, my peace I give unto you . . . ." Jesus offers us peace, not as the world gives, but as He alone gives. We, as believers, can accept His peace or ignore it. When we accept God's peace, we are blessed; when we ignore it, we suffer unfortunate and sometimes tragic consequences.

Today, as a gift to yourself, to your family, and to your students, claim the inner peace that is your spiritual birthright: the peace of Jesus Christ. It is offered freely; it has been paid for in full; it is yours for the asking. So ask. And then share.

Peace with God is where all peace begins.

Jim Gallery

What peace can they have
who are not at peace with God?

Matthew Henry

When we learn to say a deep,
passionate yes to the things that
really matter, then peace begins
to settle onto our lives like golden sunlight
sifting to a forest floor.

Thomas Kinkade

Peace is the deepest thing a human
personality can know; it is almighty.

Oswald Chambers

Christ alone can bring lasting peace—
peace with God—peace among men
and nations—and peace within our hearts.

Billy Graham

Let's please God by actively seeking,
through prayer, "peaceful and quiet lives"
for ourselves, our spouses, our children and
grandchildren, our friends, and our nation
(1 Timothy 2:1-3 NIV).

Shirley Dobson

That peace, which has been described
and which believers enjoy, is a participation
of the peace which their glorious
Lord and Master himself enjoys.

Jonathan Edwards

*But the wisdom that comes from heaven
is first of all pure; then peace-loving, considerate,
submissive, full of mercy and good fruit,
impartial and sincere.*

James 3:17 NIV

Chapter 23

A Purpose for Today, Purpose for Eternity

I know whom I have believed,
and am convinced that he is able to guard
what I have entrusted to him for that day.
2 Timothy 1:12 NIV

The familiar words of Psalm 118 remind us that today, like every day, is a priceless gift from God. And as teachers, we are doubly blessed: we can celebrate the glory of God's creation *and* we can celebrate the precious students that He has entrusted to our care.

What do you expect from the day ahead? Are you expecting God to do wonderful things, or are you living beneath a cloud of apprehension and doubt. Do you expect God to use you in unexpected ways, or do you expect another uneventful day to pass with little fanfare? As a thoughtful believer, the answer to these questions should be obvious.

For Christian believers, every new day offers exciting possibilities. God's Word promises that Christ has come to this earth to give us abundant life and eternal salvation. We, in turn, should respond to God's gifts by treasuring each day and using our time here on earth to glorify our Creator and share the Good News of His Son.

Each day is a special gift from God, a treasure to be savored and celebrated.

May we—as believers who have so much to celebrate—never fail to praise our Creator by rejoicing in His glorious creation.

———

How completely satisfying to turn
from our limitations to a God who has
none. Eternal years lie in his heart.
For him time does not pass, it remains;
and those who are in Christ share
with him all the riches of
limitless time and endless years.

A. W. Tozer

In heaven we shall "know fully."
While we were on earth, we scratched
our heads and wondered how the matted
mesh of threads in Romans 8:28 could
possibly be woven together for our good.

Joni Eareckson Tada

The unfolding of our friendship
with the Father will be a never-ending
revelation stretching on into eternity.

Catherine Marshall

Knowing where you are going takes
the uncertainty out of getting there.

Anne Graham Lotz

Jesus intended for us to be overwhelmed
by the blessings of regular days.
He said it was the reason he had come:
"I am come that they might have life,
and that they might have it
more abundantly."

Gloria Gaither

Chapter 24

And Finally . . .

*I urge you to live a life worthy
of the calling you have received.*
Ephesians 4:1 NIV

As you begin the next stage of your life's journey, consider these time-tested principles for finding your purpose in everyday life. May God richly bless you and your family as you continue on your path.

Remember That the Search for Purpose Is a Journey, Not a Destination: Amid your changing circumstances, God will continue to reveal Himself to you *if* you sincerely seek His will. As you journey through the stages of life, remember that every new day presents fresh opportunities to seek God's will; make the conscious effort to seize those opportunities.

Pray Early and Often: Start each day with a time of prayer and devotional readings. In those quiet moments, God will lead you; your task, of course, is to be still, to seek His will, and to follow His direction.

Quiet Please: Sometimes, God speaks to you in a quiet voice; usually, the small quiet voice inside can help you find the right path for your life; listen to that voice.

Use All the Tools That God Provides: As you continue to make important decisions about your future, read God's Word every day and consult with trusted advisors whom God has seen fit to place along your path.

Take Sensible Risks in Pursuit of Personal or Professional Growth: It is better to attempt noble undertakings and fail than to attempt nothing and succeed. But, make sure to avoid *foolish* risks. When in doubt, reread Proverbs.

Expect Setbacks: Your path will have many twists and turns. When you face a setback, don't become discouraged. When you encounter a roadblock, be prepared to make a U-turn. Then, start searching for a better route to your chosen destination.

Use Your Experiences As Valued Instructors: Philosopher George Santayana correctly observed, "Those who cannot remember the past are condemned to repeat it." Act accordingly.

Write It Down: If you're facing a big decision, or if you're searching for greater fulfillment from your everyday life, begin keeping a daily journal. During quiet moments, make a written record of your thoughts, your goals, your hopes, and your concerns. The simple act of writing down your thoughts will help you clarify your ideas and your plans.

Don't Settle for Second, Third, or Fourth Best: God has big plans for you. Don't let Him down.

Serve Where You Stand: Even if you're not where you want to be, you can serve God exactly where you are. So don't underestimate the importance of your present work, and don't wait for a better day to serve God.

Find Pursuits About Which You Are Passionate: Find work that you love and causes that you believe in. You'll do your best when you become so wrapped up in something that you forget to call it work.

Have Faith and Get Busy: The Lord has promised to do His part. The rest is up to you.

———

All that is not eternal is eternally out of date.

C. S. Lewis

Rejoice, and be exceeding glad:
for great is your reward in heaven . . . .

Matthew 5:12 NKJV